THIS CANDLEWICK BOOK BELONGS TO:

_____

_____

_____

For Joseph and Gabriel
who were tiny and grew big —N. D.

WRITTEN BY NICOLA DAVIES

For Lex and Kit —E. S.

Text copyright © 2014 by Nicola Davies. Illustrations copyright © 2014 by Emily Sutton. All rights reserved. No part of this book may be reproduced, transmitted, or stored in an information retrieval system in any form or by any means, graphic, electronic, or mechanical, including photocopying, taping, and recording, without prior written permission from the publisher. First U.S. paperback edition 2016. Library of Congress Catalog Card Number 2013953401. ISBN 978-0-7636-7315-4 (hardcover) ISBN 978-0-7636-8904-9 (paperback). This book was typeset in Gill Sans MT. The illustrations were done in watercolor. Candlewick Press, 99 Dover Street, Somerville, Massachusetts 02144. visit us at www.candlewick.com. Printed in Shenzhen, Guangdong, China.   22 23 24 25 CCP 12 11 10 9

TINY CREATURES

The World of Microbes

ILLUSTRATED BY EMILY SUTTON

CANDLEWICK PRESS

You know about big animals,

and you know about small animals . . .

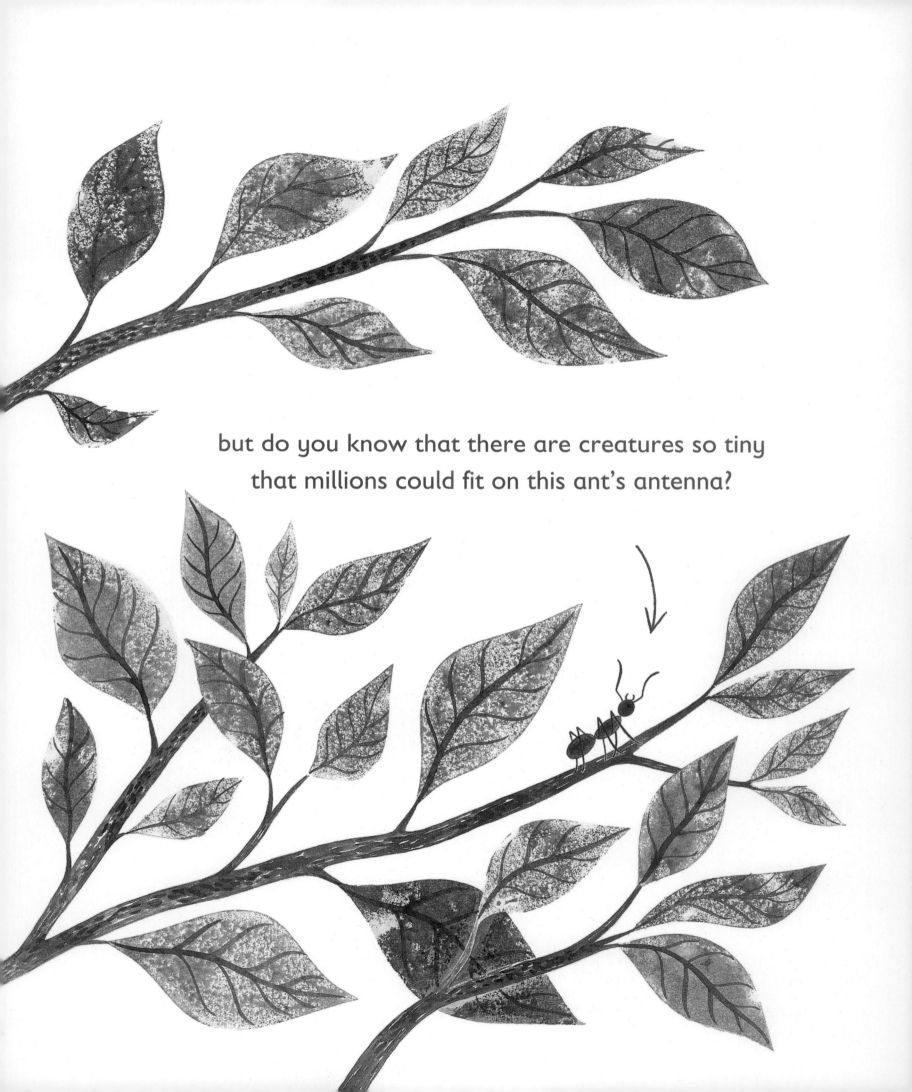

but do you know that there are creatures so tiny
that millions could fit on this ant's antenna?

So tiny that we'd have to make the ant's antenna
as big as a whale to show them to you?

ANTENNA

They don't have eyes, heads, or legs, branches, roots, or leaves because they aren't animals or plants. But they are alive.

They are called microbes, and there are lots of them.

A single drop of seawater can hold twenty million microbes. That's about the same as the number of people in New York State.

And a teaspoon of soil can have as many as a **billion** microbes. That's about the same as the number of people in the whole of India.

Microbes live everywhere—in the sea, on land, in the soil, and in the air. They live in places where nothing else does, like in volcanoes, or inside rocks, or at the back of your fridge.

They also live on the outside and inside of plants and animals.

Right now there are more microbes living on your skin than there are people on Earth, and there are ten or even a hundred times as many as that in your stomach.

(Don't worry! Although some microbes make you sick, the ones that live in you and on you all the time help keep you well.)

But even though they are too small to see, they are not all the same. There are lots of different kinds, more than there are different kinds of animals and plants. Some are tinier than others, as different in size as ants and whales.

POLIO VIRUS

One of the smallest microbes

PARAMECIUM *2,000 times bigger than the polio virus*

Some microbes are round.

Some are skinny.

Some look like shells.

Some are squishy.

Some have wiggling tails.

Some look like daisies.

Some look like spaceships.

Some look like necklaces.

Microbes can eat anything: plants, animals (alive or dead), even oil and rocks. They're too small to have mouths, so they just soak up what they need through their skin.

MENU
PLANTS
—
ANIMALS
—
ROCKS
—
OIL

That's why the things microbes eat
don't disappear in bites. They change,
slowly, into something else. . . .

FOOD *INTO* COMPOST

MILK *INTO* YOGURT

ROCKS *INTO* SOIL

And when microbes are well fed, they are really,
really good at making more microbes.
They simply split, so that where there was one,

twenty minutes later, there are two . . .

and then four,

and then eight,

and then sixteen.

Starting with just one microbe of a type
called E. coli, which of course would be far
too small for you to see, it would take eleven
and a half hours for there to be enough E. coli

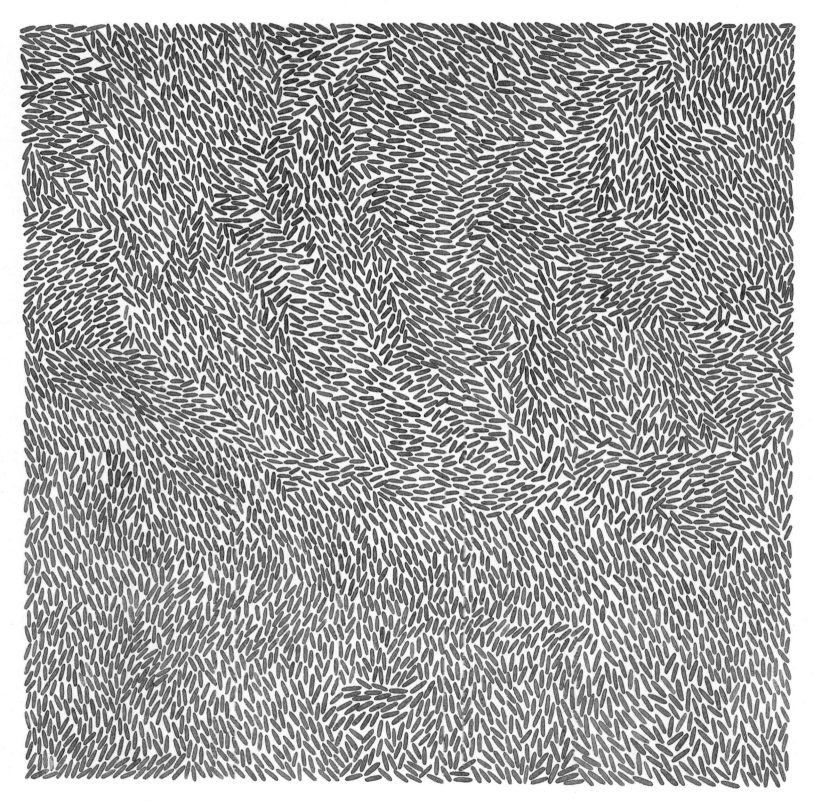

to fill this space, and twenty minutes later . . .

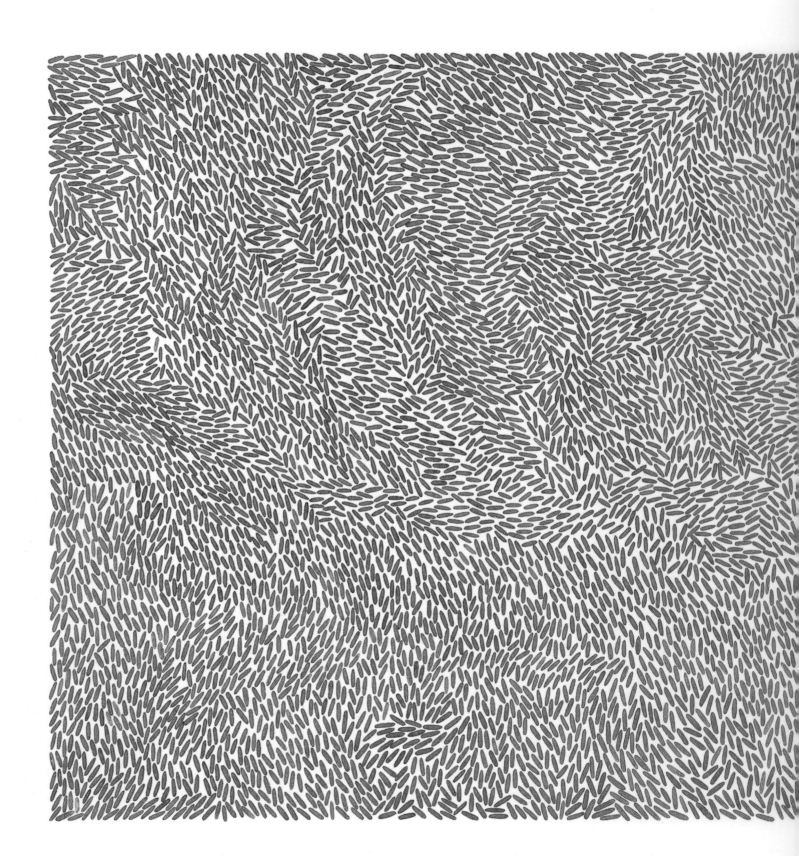

they would all split and

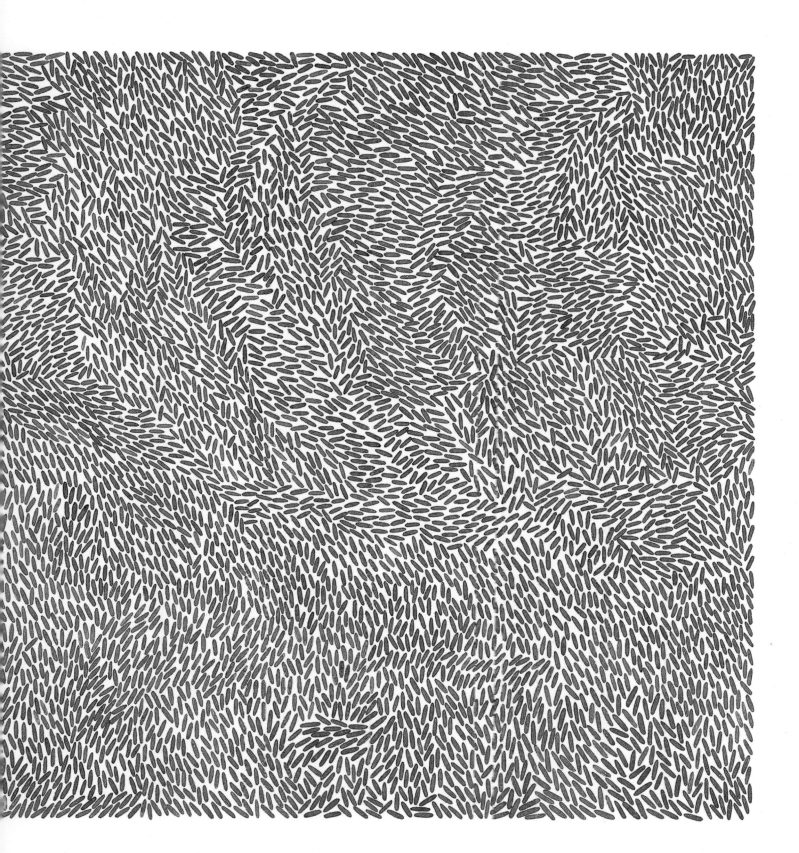

double, to fill this space.

That's why it takes only a few
of the wrong kind of microbes—
the kind we call germs—
to get into your body to make you sick.

← MOSQUITO

They get in through
your mouth or through a cut
or sometimes through an insect's bite.
Then, inside you, where they are warm and well fed,
they split and split and split until just a few germs
have turned into thousands, then millions.
They're still tiny, but there are enough
of them to make you sick.

So it's best to stop them from getting in.

Luckily, only a few kinds of microbes can make humans sick.
Most microbes are busy doing other things.

And because microbes are so
good at making more microbes,
some of the things they do
are very, very big.

They can wear down mountains
and build up cliffs.
They can stain the sea red,
turn the sky cloudy,
and make snowflakes grow.

They recycle everything that dies to make soil so that new life can sprout, and they help to make our air good to breathe.

All over the earth,
all the time, tiny microbes
are eating and eating,
and splitting and splitting,
changing one thing into another.
They are the invisible
transformers of our world—

the tiniest lives doing some
of the biggest jobs.

Nicola Davies is a zoologist and an award-winning author whose many books for children include *Bat Loves the Night*, *Dolphin Baby!*, and *I (Don't) Like Snakes*. About *Tiny Creatures*, she says, "There are so many things in our world that depend on microbes, from my favorite food — yogurt — to the air we breathe! I really wanted to tell children about these astonishing life-forms that are all around us but are so small we can't even see them." Nicola Davies lives in Wales.

Emily Sutton has a degree in illustration from Edinburgh College of Art. She says, "Illustrating *Tiny Creatures* has opened my eyes to the incredible and unexpected beauty of a world so small that it can't be seen without a microscope. I was amazed by the variety and complexity of microbes, and I loved drawing all of their intricate details and patterns." Emily Sutton lives in York, England.